W9-BEE-040

SPECTACULAR
SPACE SCIENCE

Exploring the
OUTER
PLANETS

Nancy Dickmann

rosen publishing's
rosen
central

New York

Published in 2016 by The Rosen Publishing Group, Inc.
29 East 21st Street
New York, NY 10010

Copyright © 2016 by The Rosen Publishing Group, Inc.

First Edition

All rights reserved. No part of this book may be reproduced in any form without permission in writing from the publisher, except by a reviewer.

Produced for Rosen by Calcium
Editors for Calcium: Sarah Eason and Jennifer Sanderson
Designer: Greg Tucker
Consultant: David Hawksett

Photo credits: Cover courtesy of NASA; p. 4 © Dreamstime/Mopic; p. 5 courtesy of Wikimedia Commons/ Don Davis; p. 6 © Dreamstime/Abxyz; p. 7 courtesy of Wikimedia Commons/Jean-Pol Grandmont; p. 8 courtesy of Wikimedia Commons/Justus Sustermans; p. 9 © Shutterstock/Renata Sedmakova; p. 10 © Dreamstime/Georgios Kollidas; p. 11 top courtesy of Wikimedia Commons/Geographicus Rare Antique Maps; p. 11 bottom courtesy of Wikimedia Commons/Magnus Manske; p. 12 courtesy of NASA Ames; p. 13 courtesy of Wikimedia Commons/NASA; p. 14 courtesy of NASA; pp. 16–17 courtesy of NASA/JPL/ DLR; p. 18 courtesy of NASA, JPL, Galileo Project, (NOAO), J. Burns (Cornell) et al.; p. 19 top courtesy of NASA/JPL/Cornell University; p. 19 bottom © Shutterstock/Elenarts; p. 20 courtesy of NASA/JPL-Caltech; p. 21 courtesy of NASA/ESA/AOES; p. 22 courtesy of NASA/JPL-Caltech/Space Science Institute; p. 23 top courtesy of NASA/JPL/Space Science Institute; p. 23 bottom courtesy of NASA; p. 24 NASA/JPL-Caltech/Space Science Institute; p. 25 © Shutterstock/Manamana; p. 26 courtesy of NASA/Cassini Imaging Team/Space Science institute/JPL/ESA; p. 27 courtesy of Wikimedia Commons/NASA/JPL/Space Science Institute; p. 29 courtesy of ESA/C. Carreau; p. 31 top courtesy of NASA/Cassini Imaging Team/SSI/JPL/ ESA/NASA; p. 31 bottom courtesy of NASA/JPL/Space Science Institute; p. 32 courtesy of NASA/JPL; p. 33 © Shutterstock/Tristan3D; p. 34 courtesy of NASA/JPL; pp. 34–35 courtesy of Wikimedia Commons/ NASA; p. 36 © Dreamstime/Nicholas Burningham; p. 37 courtesy of NASA; p. 38 courtesy of NASA; p. 39 courtesy of NASA/JPL-Caltech; p. 40 © Dreamstime/Rolffimages; p. 41 courtesy of NASA/JPL/DLR; p. 42 courtesy of NASA/JPL; p. 43 courtesy of Johns Hopkins University Applied Physics Laboratory/Southwest Research Institute (JHUAPL/SwRI); p. 45 © Dreamstime/Pere Sanz.

Library of Congress Cataloging-in-Publication Data

Dickmann, Nancy, author.
Exploring the outer planets/Nancy Dickmann.—First edition.
    pages cm.—(Spectacular space science)
Includes bibliographical references and index.
ISBN 978-1-4994-3633-4 (library bound)—ISBN 978-1-4994-3635-8 (pbk.)—
ISBN 978-1-4994-3636-5 (6-pack)
1. Outer planets—Juvenile literature. 2. Outer space—Exploration—Juvenile literature.
I. Title.
QB659.D53 2016
523.4—dc23

2014046807

Manufactured in the United States of America

CONTENTS

Chapter One

WELCOME TO THE SOLAR SYSTEM

We live on a large spherical rocky body, one of many that travel around the sun. The outer crust of our planet forms an incredible habitat, with fertile soils, lush rain forests, and oceans teeming with life. Earth is a wonderful place to live, and we are lucky to have it. Out of all the bodies orbiting the sun, Earth is the only one so well-suited to life. There are many different types of planets, and Earth is just one of these.

The other three planets orbiting close to the sun—Mercury, Venus, and Mars—are similar to Earth. These inner planets are fairly small and rocky, with mountains, valleys, craters, and plains. After Mars comes a very big gap, even bigger than the distance from Mars to the sun. It is not just space that separates the outer planets—Jupiter, Saturn, Uranus, and Neptune—from the inner planets. They are also completely different. Instead of being small and made of rocks and metals, these outer planets are huge balls of swirling gases, with no solid surfaces. They are surrounded by rings of ice and rock, as well as dozens of moons. They are also very cold, mainly as a result of their distance from the sun. In fact, Neptune is so far away that from there the sun just looks like a bright star.

The outer planets are separated from the inner planets by the asteroid belt, an area where many small, rocky asteroids are found.

The swirling clouds of the gas giants give them a beautiful, smooth appearance, but their moons are small and rocky and similar to the inner planets.

POOR OLD PLUTO

We used to think there were nine planets in the solar system, with Pluto being the last of the outer planets. Unlike the gas giants, Pluto is small and rocky—smaller even than Mercury. However, in 2006, the definition of a planet was changed, and Pluto was demoted to a new category: dwarf planet. Pluto is not even the biggest dwarf planet! Eris, discovered in 2005, is bigger.

Not all gas giants are created equal, though. Jupiter and Saturn, the two biggest and closest to the sun, are mainly made up of hydrogen and helium. Uranus and Neptune are smaller and colder than these two planets, and have large amounts of methane, ammonia, and water in the form of ice. In fact, they are often called "ice giants" instead of "gas giants."

Early Beliefs

You do not need a telescope to see Jupiter and Saturn, so they have been known since ancient times. Even though they look a little like stars when seen with the naked eye, early astronomers knew that they were something other than stars. The stars we see from Earth appear to rotate every twenty-four hours, but they do not change position relative to each other. The planets, on the other hand, move across the sky over a period of days, and that is how they got their name: "*planetes*" means "wanderers" in ancient Greek.

Jupiter takes about twelve years to complete one orbit of the sun. The ancient Babylonians used it to define the twelve constellations of their zodiac system. The ancient Greeks named it after Zeus, the ruler of their gods. Jupiter was the most powerful of the Roman gods, so the Romans gave his name to the biggest planet, and it is still so-named today. Jupiter seemed to rule the skies because of the way it moved through one of the twelve zodiac constellations each year. It is one of the brightest objects in the sky, and in many cultures this was seen as a sign of good luck.

The Roman god Jupiter was also known as "Jove," and this is where we get the adjective "Jovian." Jupiter and its moons are often referred to as "the Jovian system" and "Jovian planets" describes the gas giants.

Saturn was also observed by Babylonian astronomers, who associated it with their sun god, Shamash. The ancient Greeks believed it was sacred to the god Kronos, the father of Zeus and the god of agriculture. The Romans had a god named Saturn, who was considered to be the equivalent of Kronos, so they gave his name to the planet. In Greek mythology, Kronos was the son of Ouranos, who would later have the planet Uranus named after him.

The Roman god Saturn was celebrated every December with a festival called Saturnalia. People gave gifts and shared feasts, and masters traded roles with their slaves.

DIFFERENT NAMES

Although English is widely used by professional astronomers, the planets do have different names in many languages. For example, in Greece they still call Jupiter and Saturn by the names of their own ancient gods: Zeus and Kronos. Their names in Mandarin translate as "Star of Wood" (Jupiter) and "Star of Soil" (Saturn).

Observing Jupiter and Saturn

The first known telescope was invented in the early seventeenth century. The earliest version could magnify things about three times, and was seen as a fascinating novelty. The Italian astronomer Galileo Galilei (1564–1642) was the first person to realize that telescopes could be useful for studying the skies. He made his own telescopes and soon had a version that was more powerful than anything else available. He started to use it to look at Jupiter and soon discovered something amazing: Jupiter had four moons. Galileo had found the first known moons in the solar system, other than Earth's moon.

About fifty years later, Jean-Dominique Cassini (1625–1712) used an even more powerful telescope to see the spots and colored bands on Jupiter's surface. He also noticed that Jupiter appeared slightly oval, as though it were squished at its poles. He may have seen the Great Red Spot, but the first confirmed sighting was by the German astronomer Samuel Heinrich Schwabe (1789–1875) in 1831.

When Galileo used his telescope to look at Saturn, the planet looked like it had handles on each side. Galileo thought they might be moons, but he never figured out what they actually were. In 1655, the Dutch scientist Christiaan Huygens (1629–1695) was the first to realize they were rings. He also discovered Titan, the first of Saturn's moons. Huygens thought that the rings were a single solid disc, but other astronomers proved him wrong. Cassini found a large gap in the rings, and James Clerk Maxwell (1831–1879) proved in 1857 that the rings must be made up of a huge number of tiny particles.

In addition to discovering Jupiter's moons, Galileo also observed the phases of Venus and made careful studies of sunspots.

THE SPEED OF LIGHT

In 1676, the Danish astronomer Ole Rømer (1644–1710) used Jupiter's moons to calculate the speed of light. Cassini had published tables that predicted the movements of Jupiter's moons. However, when Jupiter was at its farthest point from Earth, the predictions were off by about seventeen minutes. Before this, people thought that we saw things at the same time as they happened. Rømer realized that light takes time to travel, and he used Cassini's tables to estimate the speed of light.

This tower at the University of Padua in Italy is often called "Galileo's Observatory." Many astronomers of the seventeenth century would have observed the skies from towers like this one.

Finding More Planets

Aside from Earth, only five planets were known to the ancients. Uranus is just visible to the naked eye, but to see it you have to have really good eyesight, very dark skies, and know exactly where to look. It was spotted several times in the eighteenth century by astronomers who thought it was a star. It was not until 1781 that William Herschel (1738–1822) realized that Uranus was actually a planet. He had been making a survey of stars, and found that one seemed different. It was moving too much for a star, but too slowly for a comet. After doing some calculations, he realized that he had found a new planet.

Uranus was the first planet discovered with a telescope, but Neptune was the first planet to be found using mathematics. By 1846, Uranus had made nearly one orbit of the sun since its discovery. Seeing its full orbit had made astronomers notice some irregularities in its path. They wondered what could be causing these anomalies, which did not match up with predictions based on Newton's Laws of Motion.

William Herschel was born in Germany but spent his adult life in England. He discovered several moons, as well as infrared radiation.

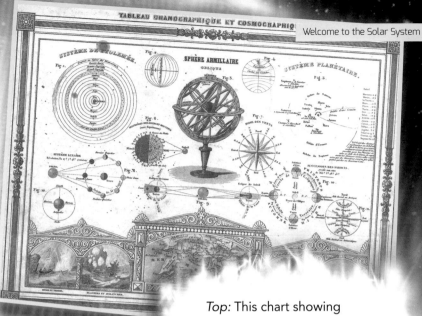

One possible explanation was that there was yet another planet beyond Uranus, whose gravity could be disrupting its orbit. Two astronomers— Urbain Le Verrier (1811–1877) in Paris and John Couch Adams (1819–1892) in England—started working on calculations to predict where this mystery planet could be. Once Le Verrier's calculations were complete, Johann Gottfried Galle (1812–1910) used them and found Neptune with his telescope, almost exactly where Le Verrier had said it would be.

Top: This chart showing objects in the sky was published in 1852. It is one of the earliest charts to include Neptune and Uranus.

Bottom: Urbain Le Verrier was a brilliant mathematician who used complicated calculations to analyze the orbits of planets, moons, and comets.

FIT FOR A KING

When Uranus was discovered, many names were proposed for the new planet. Herschel suggested "Georgium Sidus" (meaning "The Georgian Planet") in honor of King George III of Great Britain, but this was not popular in other countries. The German astronomer Johann Bode (1747–1826) suggested Uranus, a version of the name of the Greek god of the sky. In mythology, Saturn was the father of Jupiter, and Uranus (Ouranos) was the father of Saturn. The name stuck.

Chapter Two

JUPITER

In the early days of space exploration, in the 1960s, attention was focused on things that were fairly close and easy to reach, such as the moon, Venus, and Mars. Jupiter, on the other hand, is a long way away. Even when it is at its closest point to Earth, it is still more than eleven times as far away as Mars. The first space probe to approach Jupiter was Pioneer 10 in 1973. Since then, other probes have visited and sent back amazing images as well as useful data.

Pioneer 11 was launched on April 5, 1973, and flew past Jupiter on its way to Saturn. The two probes returned the first-ever close-up photographs of Jupiter and its largest moons. They also studied its atmosphere and detected its magnetic field. The information they sent back helped scientists design new probes that could cope with the conditions near Jupiter.

After visiting Jupiter and Saturn, Pioneer 11 headed out toward interstellar space. Contact with the probe was lost in 1995.

Voyagers 1 and 2 flew past Jupiter in 1979, discovering Jupiter's rings and two new moons, and taking close-up images of the planet's atmosphere. Their data proved that the Great Red Spot is actually a giant storm. The Cassini probe, which flew past Jupiter on its way to Saturn in 2000, took about twenty-six thousand detailed images.

So far, the most detailed study of Jupiter has been done by the Galileo spacecraft, the only probe to enter orbit around the planet. Launched in 1989, Galileo entered Jupiter's orbit in 1995 and stayed there for more than seven years, making thirty-four complete circuits. During this time it was able to learn about the composition of Jupiter's clouds, volcanic activity on Jupiter's moon Io, the magnetic field around Ganymede (another of Jupiter's moons), the formation of Jupiter's rings, and much more.

A HELPING HAND

All missions on their way to the outer planets are carefully timed so that they fly past Jupiter on their way to the outer solar system. The reason for this is simple: Jupiter is a massive planet, with a strong gravitational pull. With the right trajectory, spacecraft are able to use Jupiter's gravity to boost their speed. This means that they need to carry less fuel.

This artist's impression shows Galileo observing Jupiter's moon Io. The probe was able to study the planet's largest moons.

What Is Inside Jupiter?

Jupiter is truly huge. Not only is it the biggest planet, but its mass is also two-and-a-half times the mass of all the other planets combined. Unlike Earth, which is solid, it is made up mainly of gas and liquid. It is mostly hydrogen and helium, just like a star. However, Jupiter does not glow like a star because it is not big enough for the nuclear processes that take place within stars to occur.

Although we call Jupiter a gas giant, it is not completely made of gas. At its core, there is a huge amount of pressure, and scientists believe that it is likely to be a thick, super-hot mixture of rock and hydrogen. There is probably also a layer of liquid hydrogen and helium. We cannot really state confidently what Jupiter is like on the inside, but astronomers make educated guesses based on the information they have at the time.

Unlike Earth, on Jupiter there is no clear boundary between the atmosphere and the rest of the planet. However, as you get closer to the core of the planet, the density and temperature of the gases change, allowing scientists to divide it into distinct layers. Within this atmosphere are hundreds of swirling clouds and storms, including the Great Red Spot.

Jupiter may be the biggest planet, but it is also the fastest spinner: it rotates about once every ten hours. This incredibly fast rotation makes the planet bulge out at the equator. Scientists were able to time radio signals coming from Jupiter in 1955 to calculate its rotation rate.

Jupiter's Great Red Spot is actually a giant storm that has lasted for hundreds of years. The storm's diameter is about one-and-a-third times the diameter of Earth.

CRASH LANDING

In 1994, scientists could see below Jupiter's cloud tops. Comet Shoemaker-Levy 9 had been discovered in orbit around Jupiter in 1993. It had probably been captured by Jupiter's gravity years before, and had eventually been torn into pieces by it. From July 16, 1994 to July 22, 1994, the comet's fragments smashed into Jupiter at about 134,000 miles per hour (215,652 kilometers per hour), leaving a chain of "bruises" that lasted for months.

Moons

Jupiter has more than sixty moons, and the four largest are the ones discovered by Galileo more than four hundred years ago. They are still called the Galilean moons in his honor. They stand out in many ways: they were the first moons of another planet to be discovered; they are some of the biggest moons in the solar system; and they are much bigger than any of the other moons orbiting Jupiter.

Ganymede, the largest, is a true giant of a moon, even bigger than the planet Mercury. If it were orbiting the sun instead of Jupiter, it would probably be considered a planet. Like all of Jupiter's moons, it is made of rock and ice, not gas. Based on data from the Galileo probe, astronomers believe that beneath its surface is an ocean of liquid, salty water.

Europa

Io

Jupiter

Jupiter's moons never actually line up this neatly, but here you can see them arranged by distance from the planet.

Callisto

Ganymede

NAMING MOONS

Astronomers often turn to mythology to name moons and other objects. Jupiter's moons are named after characters in Greek mythology who are associated with Zeus, the Greek equivalent of Jupiter. The first moons of Saturn to be discovered were named after the brothers and sisters of Saturn in mythology. When astronomers kept discovering moons but ran out of siblings, they began to name them after giants from the mythology of other cultures.

Next in size is Callisto, which is slightly smaller than Mercury, but much less dense. It is also made of rock and ice, and its surface is covered in craters. It is believed to be one of the oldest surfaces in the solar system, because there is no evidence of volcanoes or shifting tectonic plates to alter the crust. Io, on the other hand, is completely different. It has more than four hundred active volcanoes, which shoot out jets of sulfurous compounds and lava. Their lava flows have left the surface brightly colored in shades of yellow, red, green, white, and black.

Europa is the smallest of the Galilean moons, and possibly the most interesting. Scientists believe that it has a rocky core surrounded by a massive ocean of liquid water, topped with a thick icy crust. The crust is crisscrossed with cracks.

17

Smaller Moons

Although the Galilean moons are fascinating, Jupiter has dozens of other moons, most discovered fairly recently. Before 2000, astronomers only knew of seventeen moons orbiting Jupiter. In 2011, they discovered the sixty-seventh, and it is likely that there are more to be found. Most of the non-Galilean moons are very small—fewer than 6.2 miles (10 km) in diameter—which makes them hard to find. Very powerful ground-based telescopes were used to track them down.

Metis, Adrastea, Amalthea, and Thebe are known as the inner moons. They orbit closer to Jupiter than the four Galilean moons, and are larger than the majority of Jupiter's moons. Their orbits are nearly circular and they orbit close to the planet's equator, in contrast to the dozens of smaller moons, which have highly eccentric orbits. Astronomers believe that many of them are captured objects. This notion means that instead of forming around the same time as Jupiter did (like the Galilean moons), they were asteroids, comets, or other objects that were captured by Jupiter's gravity and forced into orbit around it.

JUPITER'S RINGS

Like Saturn, Jupiter also has a ring system, which was discovered by Voyager 1 in 1979. There are four thin rings made mainly of dust. Since their discovery, the rings have been studied by the Hubble Space Telescope and other telescopes on Earth. The Galileo probe found evidence that the rings were formed by dust kicked up when objects crashed into the four inner moons.

Jupiter's rings are thin and faint, and very difficult to observe.

Top: This composite image, taken by Galileo, shows (from left) Metis, Adrastea, Amalthea, and Thebe.

Bottom: The Voyager spacecraft discovered Thebe and Metis.

Jupiter's smaller moons are so little and far away that we cannot learn much about them from Earth. Several of them have been photographed by probes such as Voyager and Cassini, and a few have been studied in more detail by the Galileo probe. For example, it mapped the surfaces of Thebe and Amalthea, and sent back data about their composition. Galileo's last experiment before crashing into Jupiter was to measure the mass of Amalthea.

Future Missions

Galileo sent back a treasure trove of data about Jupiter and its moons. However, there is still more to learn, and the next discoveries will come from the Juno probe, launched in 2011 by the National Aeronautics and Space Administration (NASA). When it arrives at Jupiter in 2016, it will go into orbit around the planet's poles. Scientists hope that Juno can answer some of the questions we still have about Jupiter. For example, it will determine how much water exists in the planet's atmosphere. Knowing this amount will give us insight into how the planet was formed. Juno will also measure the temperature and composition of Jupiter's clouds.

One of the biggest parts of Juno's mission is investigating Jupiter's magnetosphere. A planet's magnetosphere is the region of space around it in which its own magnetic field deflects the "solar wind," a wave of particles coming from the sun. Not all planets have magnetospheres; for example, Venus does not. Earth's magnetosphere plays a crucial role in protecting us from harmful radiation but it cannot compare to Jupiter's enormous magnetosphere, which extends millions of miles into space. Astronomers hope that studying the magnetosphere will shed light on Jupiter's internal structure, as well as how the magnetic field affects the atmosphere.

Unlike Galileo, which studied Jupiter's moons as well as the planet itself, the Juno probe will focus its investigations on the planet.

This artist's impression shows the Jupiter Icy moons Explorer (JUICE) spacecraft next to Jupiter and Europa. It will use radar to "see" beneath the moon's icy surface.

One of the reasons the Galilean moons are so interesting is that three of them are thought to have liquid water beneath their surfaces. The European Space Agency's (ESA's) JUICE mission is scheduled to launch in 2022. It will explore Ganymede, Callisto, and Europa in more detail.

STAYING SAFE

One reason for Juno's polar orbit is that it avoids long-term contact with Jupiter's radiation belts. These are areas around Jupiter, mainly surrounding its equator, where there are high levels of radiation caused by the planet's magnetic field. The radiation can damage spacecraft and their electrical components. Even with the safer orbit, Juno's electronics must still be protected by a 0.4-inch (one-centimeter) thick wall of titanium.

21

Chapter Three

SATURN

In the seventeenth and eighteenth centuries, seven moons were discovered orbiting Saturn, and Saturn's rings were finally seen clearly. It was not until spacecraft began visiting the planet in the 1970s that we really started finding out more about Saturn. In 1979, the Pioneer 11 spacecraft was the first to visit Saturn. It took photographs of the planet and a few of its moons, as well as sending back information about its rings.

Pioneer 11 was followed by Voyager 1 in 1980 and Voyager 2 in 1981. Voyager 1 was able to send back much better images, including clear photographs of the surfaces of some of the moons. It passed fairly close to Titan and studied its atmosphere. Voyager 2 was less successful; its camera platform was stuck for a few days, so it was unable to take all of the planned photographs.

After Voyager 2, Saturn was left unvisited for more than twenty years. It was not until the Cassini-Huygens probe arrived in 2004 that scientists were able to study the planet in more detail. Cassini remained in orbit around the planet while sending the lander, Huygens, down to the solid surface of Titan. Huygens was the first spacecraft to land on a body in the outer solar system. It was able to send information about Titan's surface to Earth.

In this photograph, Saturn was in the right position to block out the sun, allowing for an amazing backlit view of Saturn's rings.

While Cassini remained in orbit, it took measurements of the planet and its rings, and carried out flybys of some of its moons. Scientists were able to use a combination of rocket firing and Titan's gravity to "tweak" Cassini's orbit over the years, allowing it to observe Saturn and its moons from a variety of positions.

Top: Cassini took this photograph of Saturn's moon Hyperion. It is not very dense and looks a little like a sponge.

Bottom: This illustration shows the Cassini probe in orbit around Saturn.

THE DAY THE EARTH SMILED

On July 19, 2013, Cassini was in a good position to take a photograph of the entire Saturn system, as well as Earth and its moon, Mars, and Venus. People on Earth were told in advance about the opportunity, and encouraged to look up and smile at the moment the photograph was taken.

23

Structure and Movement

Scientists believe that Saturn's structure is similar to that of Jupiter. It is mainly made up of hydrogen and helium, and it probably has some sort of solid core. The gases can also be found in liquid and molten states, depending on the depth toward the core. However, Saturn is not very dense. In fact, it is the least dense object that we know of in the solar system. Given a big enough ocean, Saturn would float.

When seen through a basic telescope, Saturn is a pale orange-yellow color. Seen up close, it reveals a beautiful pattern of different colored bands. The stripes are bands of clouds, and the different colors are caused by trace amounts of chemicals such as ammonia, ethane, and methane, mixed in with the hydrogen and helium. The clouds are affected by some of the strongest winds ever recorded in the solar system. When Voyager 1 visited Saturn, it measured the wind speed near the planet's equator at more than 1,100 miles per hour (1,770 km per hour).

In this false-color image of an enormous storm at Saturn's north pole, low clouds are shown in red and higher clouds are green. No one knows how long this hurricane has been active.

The Very Large Array, in New Mexico, is a telescope system that receives radio waves from distant objects. It has made several important discoveries about Saturn.

It takes Saturn more than twenty-nine Earth years to complete an orbit around the sun, but fewer than eleven hours to rotate on its axis. Figuring out the rotation speed of a gas giant is tricky, because astronomers cannot judge it based on surface features. Saturn's swirling bands of cloud are constantly in motion. Astronomers have used radio signals coming from the planet to estimate its rotation period, although different parts of the planet seem to rotate at slightly different rates. Saturn's quick rotation makes it bulge out at the center, even more than Jupiter does.

BIRTH OF A GIANT

One reason that scientists think Jupiter and Saturn must have some sort of solid core is based on their formations. The theory says that the planets must have started off as rocky or icy cores with a large mass. Otherwise they would not have had enough gravity to capture gases from space to form their outer layers.

Rings

Saturn's most recognizable feature is the series of beautiful rings that circle its equator. The rings are about 170,000 miles (273,588 km) wide, but only a few hundred feet thick. They are divided into different sections, separated by gaps. The two densest sections of the rings are the A and B rings, separated by the Cassini Division (named after the man who discovered it). As our views of Saturn have improved, the number of known rings has increased. The Cassini spacecraft has discovered more rings, and more divisions between the rings.

The rings are made up of dust, rock, and ice. Some of the rings are easily visible because they reflect sunlight, and scientists were able to analyze this light to figure out what the rings are made of. Although how they formed is subject to some debate.

When seen up close, Saturn's rings reveal a complex pattern of gaps.

BIRTH OF THE SOLAR SYSTEM

Scientists are especially interested in Saturn's rings because they may provide clues as to how the solar system was formed. In the early days of the sun, a flat disc of particles surrounded it, a little like Saturn's rings. These particles eventually started to clump together to form planets and other objects.

One theory about the rings is that they are made of fragments of a former moon. The idea is that at some point in the planet's early history, a large moon was torn into pieces by Saturn's gravity. Possibly, two moons collided, or a comet or asteroid crashed into a moon and made it shatter. However it happened, the particles left behind would eventually settle into orbit around Saturn's equator. Another theory is that the rings formed from the same solar nebula that Saturn itself formed from. That would mean they are made up of leftover material that never fell into Saturn.

Data from Voyager and the Hubble Space Telescope showed that the rings were probably fairly new. However, new readings from Cassini show that some rings are much older than others. It appears that the ring material is constantly recycled.

This is the last photograph of Saturn and its entire ring system that Cassini was able to take. After taking it, the probe moved too close to the planet to be able to get such a wide view again.

Titan

Saturn's largest moon, Titan, is a fascinating place. It is the only moon that we know of in the solar system with clouds and a thick atmosphere. It is also the only place—aside from Earth—that has liquid on its surface. However, the clouds and lakes on Titan are not made of water. The clouds are mainly nitrogen, with a little bit of methane, and the lakes are liquid methane. This composition makes Titan extremely flammable, but luckily there is no oxygen in the atmosphere, so the methane cannot catch fire.

Although Titan's thick clouds prevent astronomers from learning much about it by using telescopes, we do know a lot about the moon. This understanding is mostly thanks to Cassini-Huygens. While Cassini took readings from its position in orbit, it sent the Huygens lander to Titan's surface. Huygens landed on January 14, 2005, and transmitted data for seventy-two minutes. It sent back 350 photographs, including one that showed a shoreline and part of a river delta. Based on how Huygens landed, astronomers think that Titan's surface has a hard outer crust protecting a softer layer—a little like snow that has been frozen on top.

Part of the reason that Titan is so fascinating is the possibility that life might once have existed there, and may still exist today. Conditions on Titan are fairly similar to those that existed on Earth at the time when life first began. So far we have not found any definite proof, but there are many different theories. Titan's surface is extremely cold at -289 degrees Fahrenheit (-178 degrees Celsius), which would make it difficult for life to survive. However, there may be warmer places beneath the surface.

READY TO FLY?

Titan is not really a great place for humans to live; it is too cold, it does not have liquid water, and it does not have an atmosphere we can breathe. However, the combination of Titan's thick atmosphere and low gravity mean that humans would be able to strap on wings and fly fairly easily. That is, once the other survival problems had been solved!

Top: This artist's impression shows the Huygens lander on the surface of Titan. You can see the parachute that helped it drift down safely.

Right: Huygens sent back this photograph of the icy surface of Titan.

Other Moons of Saturn

Aside from Titan, Saturn has at least sixty other moons. Many of them are tiny and hidden within the rings; they were discovered thanks to the images sent back by Voyager 1 and 2 and Cassini. Most of the larger moons were discovered using telescopes more than one hundred years ago.

Some of the larger moons, such as Dione and Rhea, have heavily cratered surfaces, a little like the surface of Earth's moon. However, these moons also have bright patches that may be made of ice. Mimas, another of Saturn's moons, takes craters a step farther: it has one of the largest craters in relation to its size that we have ever discovered. The huge crater makes this moon look like the Death Star from the *Star Wars* movies.

Iapetus is one of the more unusual moons: it is black on one side and white on the other. The same side of Iapetus is always facing forward as it moves around Saturn, so one theory for the dark area is that it was caused by the moon picking up dust as it traveled. Some astronomers believe that the dark areas heat up more, turning ice into water vapor that then freezes into new white ice as it passes the colder, white area of Iapetus.

Enceladus has a surface made up almost solely of water ice. It does not have many craters, and Cassini has provided evidence that the moon is geologically active. Instead of spewing out molten rock, the "volcanoes" on Enceladus are spewing out ice and water vapor. Some of this ice has formed a ring around Saturn. Scientists believe that areas of Enceladus' surface have melted and refrozen fairly recently.

A CONNECTED SYSTEM

It is hard to tell where Saturn's moons stop and the rings begin. The smallest moons are not much larger than the chunks of matter in the rings, and they are located within the rings. For this reason, most astronomers consider Saturn's rings and moons to form a single system.

Iapetus is black on one side and white on the other, so to early astronomers it seemed to disappear from time to time.

In this Cassini photograph you can see a jet of ice spewing out of one of Enceladus' volcanoes.

31

Chapter Four

URANUS AND NEPTUNE

Compared with the other planets, we know little about Uranus and Neptune. They have been visited by only one spacecraft: Voyager 2 flew past Uranus in 1986 and Neptune in 1989. The probe was able to take photographs of both planets and their moons. These are the only clear photographs that we have.

At its closest point to Earth, Uranus is nearly 1.7 billion miles (2.7 billion km) away, and Neptune is even farther: about 2.7 billion miles (4.3 billion km). There is a limit to how much we can learn from telescopes based on Earth when pointing at something so far away. For example, before Voyager 2 visited Uranus, astronomers knew that it had rings and moons, but they did not know how many or what they were made of. They knew the planet's average temperature, but that was all. Voyager 2 revealed fifteen moons and eleven rings, as well as information about the planet's atmosphere and magnetic field.

The Voyager 2 spacecraft vastly increased our knowledge of the outer planets. It is now heading out of the solar system, but is still in contact with scientists on Earth.

GETTING A CLOSER LOOK

Telescopes in orbit around Earth are still very far from Uranus and Neptune, but they get a clearer view. This perspective is because they do not have to peer through Earth's thick atmosphere. The Hubble Space Telescope, launched in 1990, found two new moons and two rings around Uranus that Voyager had not spotted.

This artist's impression of Uranus shows its beautiful, pale-blue color.

Luckily, there are other ways of "looking" at planets. Light and energy come in many forms, and each can tell us something different. For example, infrared is part of the spectrum that we cannot see as visible light. The Keck telescope in Hawaii was designed to pick up infrared radiation, and in 2000 it used this information to produce images of giant storms on Neptune. The storms were caused by heat coming from Neptune's core.

Based on the data we have, we know that Uranus and Neptune are similar in size and are made up of the same substances. Their atmospheres are mainly hydrogen, helium, and methane. The methane gives these planets their distinctive blue color. The similarities extend to their temperatures: both are about 890 degrees Fahrenheit (477 degrees C) at their cloud tops.

33

Structure and Movement

Scientists believe that both planets have solid cores about the same size as Earth, made of molten rock and metal. Outside that they have liquid layers, which eventually merge into the gaseous layers of the atmosphere. One way that scientists learn about the interiors of these distant planets is by looking at centrifugal force. This centrifugal force is the force that pulls something traveling in a curved path away from the center of rotation. When a planet rotates, matter that is fluid (not solid) will be pushed away from the center. By using detailed measurements taken by Voyager 2, scientists can test out computer models to see what structure matches best with the readings.

Both Uranus and Neptune have magnetic fields, but they are unusual. Most planets' magnetic fields are aligned around an axis that is fairly similar to each planet's rotational axis. However, for Uranus and Neptune, the magnetic field's axis is completely different. This variation may mean that the magnetic fields are generated far from the planets' cores.

STORMY WEATHER

One main difference between Uranus and Neptune is that Uranus's atmosphere is fairly quiet, while the surface of Neptune swirls with storms and fast-moving clouds. Winds have been measured on Neptune at 1,300 miles per hour (2,092 km per hour)— faster than any other winds in the solar system. One possible reason for Uranus being so much quieter is its unusual tilt.

This white shape on the surface of Neptune is actually a fast-moving patch of cloud, nicknamed the "Scooter."

Uranus and Neptune are so far from the sun that their orbits are incredibly long. Uranus takes more than eighty-four Earth years to travel around the sun. Neptune takes 165 years. In fact, it was only in 2011 that Neptune completed the first full circuit of the sun since its discovery. The two planets rotate fairly quickly, though. Neptune rotates about every sixteen hours, and Uranus every seventeen hours. However, Uranus's rotation is very unusual. Most planet's axes are tilted a little, but Uranus's axis is tilted so much that the planet is effectively tipped over on its side. This angle means that its north pole gets constant sunlight for forty-two years, followed by forty-two years of darkness.

If you compare this view of Uranus and its ring system with photographs of Saturn, you can see why astronomers say that the planet is tipped over on its side.

Rings and Moons

Like the other two gas giants, both Uranus and Neptune are circled by moons and rings. Uranus has twenty-seven known moons and at least ten rings, and Neptune has thirteen moons and at least six narrow rings. As with Saturn, the moons and rings form part of a single interconnected system. The rings of Uranus were discovered by accident in 1977. Astronomers were watching as Uranus passed in front of a star, temporarily blocking its light. They were surprised to see the star dim five times before and after the body of the planet passed in front of it. This occurance showed that the planet was surrounded by five faint rings.

Uranus's largest moons were discovered through telescopes on Earth, and Voyager 2 found ten moons around Uranus when it visited. Some of its moons, including all of the bigger ones, orbit fairly close to the planet, in regular-shaped orbits. It is likely that they were formed around the same time as the planet itself. The outer moons are small and have eccentric orbits, and astronomers believe that they were captured by Uranus's gravity.

This artist's impression shows Neptune "rising" over the surface of its largest moon, Triton.

Voyager 2 took this photograph of Triton's icy surface.

WHAT'S IN A NAME?

Uranus's moons have one thing that sets them apart from the other moons in the solar system. Instead of being named after characters from myths and legends, they are named after characters from plays by William Shakespeare (1564–1616) and a poem by Alexander Pope (1688–1744). Neptune was the Roman god of the sea, so its moons are named after characters associated with him or with water.

The moons of Neptune follow a similar pattern. The inner moons travel in nearly circular orbits around Neptune's equator, and the tiny outer moons have more eccentric orbits. One moon, Triton, dominates the others. It is more than six times as big as the next-biggest moon, with a diameter nearly as wide as Earth's moon. Triton is unusual because it orbits Neptune in the opposite direction to the planet's rotation. Its orbit is also highly tilted. These two features make it likely that it formed elsewhere in the solar system and was captured by Neptune's gravity.

Chapter Five

WHAT'S NEXT?

The past forty years have seen our knowledge of the outer solar system increase exponentially. Scientists have discovered dozens of new moons, as well as rings circling Jupiter, Uranus, and Neptune. Spacecraft have sent back data about the planets' structures, atmospheres, and magnetic fields. At the same time, telescopes on Earth have used different wavelengths of energy to learn more. Some of these discoveries have helped us develop a clearer picture of how the solar system formed.

However, there is always more to learn. Cassini is still sending back new discoveries from the Saturn system, and Juno will soon do the same for Jupiter. Every discovery adds to the wealth of knowledge we have about the gas giants.

The Hubble Space Telescope orbits Earth, and from its vantage point it can get clear images of the outer solar system.

There are some fascinating mysteries still to be solved about the outer planets. For example, did life once exist on any of the icy moons that orbit them, and is there still life today? What is the cause of the massive ridge of mountains that runs three-quarters of the way around the equator of Iapetus? What is causing the cracks on Europa's surface? Why do Io's volcanoes not match up with where we believe the hottest underground locations to be?

One particularly mysterious place is Miranda, one of the moons of Uranus. It has a bizarre appearance, with broken terrain, huge canyons, and large grooves that do not look like they all belong on the same moon. These features would be normal on a planet that has shifting tectonic plates, like Earth, but Miranda is much too small for that. Scientists are still trying to figure out what gave Miranda its unusual appearance.

EXOPLANETS

In recent years, astronomers have been finding hundreds of exoplanets, which are planets that orbit stars other than the sun. They are all very far away and difficult to study. However, we can tell that many of them are gas giants like Jupiter. The team behind the Juno mission hopes that its discoveries can help astronomers understand more about exoplanets.

One theory about Miranda's appearance is that at some point it was hit by another object and broke apart, before gravity pulled it clumsily back together.

39

Could We Live There?

For decades, humans have been captivated by the idea of living on another planet. Some people have proposed setting up distant colonies to solve population problems on Earth, or to mine valuable natural resources and send them home. Unfortunately, it would be extremely difficult for humans to live on, or even visit, one of the gas giants. The main obstacle is the lack of a solid surface, but there are other challenges, too: extremely cold temperatures; high levels of radiation; strong winds; and powerful lightning are just a few.

However, the moons of the outer solar system are another story. They also have low temperatures, but they have solid surfaces, and many have water in the form of ice. Some of them are even believed to have liquid water beneath their surfaces. A source of water is crucial for supporting any type of human colony.

Many artists and writers have imagined what colonies on other worlds would look like. They would have to offer their residents protection from extreme temperatures and radiation.

Scientists disagree about which moon would be best for colonization. Jupiter's intense radiation could easily kill astronauts on Io or Europa, but Ganymede has a magnetosphere that provides some protection, and Callisto is far enough away to avoid most of the radiation. Saturn's moon Titan has plenty of the elements necessary to support life, and Enceladus is believed to have liquid water closer to the surface than on any other moon.

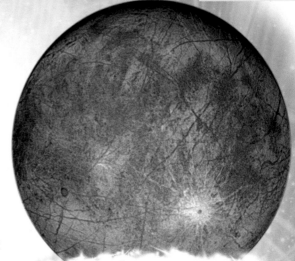

Will we ever discover what lies beneath Europa's icy surface?

Although people may never live there, these moons may already contain other forms of life. After all, there are tiny organisms on Earth that can survive in ice, on the edges of hot geysers, or in the absence of oxygen. It is not such a stretch to think that similar organisms might have evolved on Europa, Titan, or Enceladus.

ARE WE THERE YET?

One of the main problems with visiting the outer planets is their huge distance from Earth. The Juno spacecraft is taking five years to travel to Jupiter, and the New Horizons probe will take nearly ten years to reach the dwarf planet Pluto. Can you imagine how much food and water you would need to bring to feed a space crew for that long?

Future Missions

Aside from Juno, several other missions to the outer planets are in the planning stages. NASA's Europa Clipper will launch sometime in the 2020s and study Europa in detail over the course of thirty-two flybys. NASA is also planning a joint mission to Saturn with ESA. If it goes ahead, the TItan Saturn System Mission will explore Titan and Enceladus in depth.

A number of missions have been proposed to explore Uranus, but they are all awaiting funding. Sending a spacecraft on such a long journey is a huge challenge that requires careful planning and a lot of money. The different proposals include a nuclear-powered orbiter equipped with tools such as spectrometers, and a solar-powered orbiter with particle detectors and tools for measuring the magnetic field.

One of the biggest problems with sending spacecraft to the outer planets is the distance. Scientists have been working on ways to make spacecraft travel faster and use less fuel. Many current and recent missions, including Juno, have used solar power. However, the farther you get from the sun, the less useful this power is. A mission to Uranus or Neptune just would not capture enough energy from the distant sun.

Another new technology being tried out on spacecraft is the ion drive, which works by bombarding a gas (usually xenon) with electrons. When the resulting ions in the gas reach a high enough speed, they are focused into an ion beam that shoots out the back and thrusts the spacecraft forward. It uses relatively little fuel and can achieve high speeds.

An ion drive was successfully tested on the Deep Space 1 mission and is in use on the Dawn probe, which is studying asteroids.

The New Horizons probe flew past Jupiter on its way to Pluto, where it will take the first clear photographs of the dwarf planet and its moons.

POWERED BY PLUTONIUM

The New Horizons probe, on its way to Pluto, uses radioactive plutonium as a power source. This type of power eventually runs out, but it is long-lasting enough for a trip to the outer solar system. Although the mission was eventually launched successfully, some people protested against it. They were worried that an accident during the launch could release radiation into Earth's atmosphere.

43

Could It Be You?

The past years have seen such huge advances in our knowledge of the outer solar system that it is hard to predict what will be happening in another twenty or thirty years. Perhaps by then we will have seen a crewed mission to Mars, which could test out technology for a later trip to one of the outer planets or their moons. Maybe a new generation of space probes will be in orbit around Uranus or Neptune. There might be a robot rover driving across the surface of Ganymede, or a robot submarine exploring Europa's hidden oceans. The possibilities are endless!

It takes large teams of scientists, engineers, and other dedicated people to plan, design, build, and use space probes. Once a probe is launched on its journey, fixing problems is extremely difficult. Everything is calculated and recalculated, tested and retested, before a spacecraft is ready to launch. It is a thrilling and rewarding job for anyone with an interest in science.

The Earth-based tools that astronomers use to learn about distant space are improving, too. Ever more sensitive telescopes are being built on Earth, as well as being sent into orbit. The Very Large Telescope in Chile, which collects visible light as well as infrared, has been used to study Uranus. The Hubble Space Telescope has provided amazing images of the outer planets, but they are more than just pretty pictures. The information it collects has allowed astronomers to learn more about these distant worlds.

TRY IT YOURSELF

Jupiter is easy to find in the night sky, and Saturn is not too difficult either. You can download star charts or apps that will show you where to look. You do not even need a telescope! With a good pair of binoculars you should be able to see the Galilean moons, and with a fairly simple telescope, the bands of color on Jupiter will be visible. Binoculars will show you Saturn's golden color, although you will need a small telescope to see the rings.

You do not need to travel into space to see the outer planets —all you need is a clear night, binoculars, and a map!

GLOSSARY

asteroid A small, rocky, planet-like body that orbits the sun but is not big enough to be considered a planet.

astronomers People who study planets, stars, and other objects beyond Earth.

atmosphere The layer of gases surrounding a planet.

axis An imaginary line through the center of a planet, around which it rotates.

comet An icy object in space that travels in a long, looping path around the sun. Comets usually form a long, bright tail as they move through the sky.

core The center area of something, such as a planet.

craters Hollow areas, like the inside of a bowl, created when an object crashes into a planet or other large object.

crust The hard outer shell of something.

dense Having a lot of mass packed into a small space.

eccentric Not having its axis placed right at the center. Instead of being a perfect circle, an eccentric orbit is more like an oval or squished circle.

equator An imaginary line that goes around the center of a planet or moon, halfway between its two poles.

exoplanets Planets that orbit a star other than our sun.

flyby A flight past an object to make observations. When a spacecraft does a flyby of a planet, it does not stop or enter orbit.

gravity The force that pulls all objects toward each other.

infrared radiation A type of electromagnetic energy with a long wavelength that cannot be seen as visible light.

lander A spacecraft designed to land on the surface of a planet or other object and send back data.

magnetic field The space around a magnet in which a magnetic force is active.

magnetosphere The region surrounding a planet or other object in which its magnetic fields is the dominant magnetic field.

mass A measure of how much matter is in an object.

methane A gas made of carbon and hydrogen atoms bonded together.

mythology A collection of stories that form part of the traditional knowledge of a culture. Myths often try to explain how the world began and why nature behaves the way that it does.

orbit The curved path that one body in space takes around another, such as a moon orbiting a planet.

poles The ends of a planet's axis.

probe An instrument or tool used to explore something that cannot be observed directly.

radiation Waves of energy sent out by sources of heat or light, such as the sun. Radiation can be harmful to living things.

rings Flat, circular bands of small particles surrounding some planets.

rotate To spin around a central axis. The rotation of Earth is what causes night and day.

spectrometers Tools used for measuring wavelengths of light by spreading radiation into an ordered sequence.

tectonic plates Any of the segments of a planet's or moon's crust that move around in relation to one another. Movement of tectonic plates causes earthquakes and volcanoes.

water vapor Water in the form of gas.

FOR MORE INFORMATION

Books

Aguilar, David A. *Space Encyclopedia: A Tour of Our Solar System and Beyond.* Washington, D.C.: National Geographic Kids, 2013.

Graham, Ian. *What Do We Know About the Solar System?* (Earth, Space, & Beyond). Chicago, IL: Heinemann-Raintree, 2012.

Nichols, Amie. *Journey to Saturn* (Spotlight on Space Science). New York, NY: PowerKids Press, 2015.

Owen, Ruth: *Neptune* (Explore Outer Space). New York, NY: Windmill Books, 2014.

Rooney, Anne. *Outer Space* (Earth's Final Frontiers). Chicago, IL: Heinemann-Raintree, 2008.

Solway, Andrew. *Jupiter and the Outer Planets* (Astronaut Travel Guides). Chicago, IL: Heinemann-Raintree, 2014.

Websites

Due to the changing nature of Internet links, Rosen Publishing has developed an online list of websites related to the subject of this book. This site is updated regularly. Please use this link to access the list:

http://www.rosenlinks.com/SSS/Outer

INDEX

31192021426547